Appointment Book

Name: _____

Phone: _____

Email: _____

Address: _____

Name	Mobile	Email

Month: _____

	Monday	Tuesday	Wednesday	Thursday
07 AM				
08 AM				
09 AM				
10 AM				
11 AM				
12 PM				
1 PM				
2 PM				
3 PM				
4 PM				
5 PM				
6 PM				

Month: _____

	Friday	Saturday	Sunday	Note
07 AM				
08 AM				
09 AM				
10 AM				
11 AM				
12 PM				
1 PM				
2 PM				
3 PM				
4 PM				
5 PM				
6 PM				

Month: _____

	Monday	Tuesday	Wednesday	Thursday
07 AM				
08 AM				
09 AM				
10 AM				
11 AM				
12 PM				
1 PM				
2 PM				
3 PM				
4 PM				
5 PM				
6 PM				

Month: _____

	Friday	Saturday	Sunday	Note
07 AM				
08 AM				
09 AM				
10 AM				
11 AM				
12 PM				
1 PM				
2 PM				
3 PM				
4 PM				
5 PM				
6 PM				

Month: _____

	Monday	Tuesday	Wednesday	Thursday
07 AM				
08 AM				
09 AM				
10 AM				
11 AM				
12 PM				
1 PM				
2 PM				
3 PM				
4 PM				
5 PM				
6 PM				

Month: _____

	Friday	Saturday	Sunday	Note
07 AM				
08 AM				
09 AM				
10 AM				
11 AM				
12 PM				
1 PM				
2 PM				
3 PM				
4 PM				
5 PM				
6 PM				

Month: _____

	Monday	Tuesday	Wednesday	Thursday
07 AM				
08 AM				
09 AM				
10 AM				
11 AM				
12 PM				
1 PM				
2 PM				
3 PM				
4 PM				
5 PM				
6 PM				

Month: _____

	Friday	Saturday	Sunday	Note
07 AM				
08 AM				
09 AM				
10 AM				
11 AM				
12 PM				
1 PM				
2 PM				
3 PM				
4 PM				
5 PM				
6 PM				

Month: _____

	Monday	Tuesday	Wednesday	Thursday
07 AM				
08 AM				
09 AM				
10 AM				
11 AM				
12 PM				
1 PM				
2 PM				
3 PM				
4 PM				
5 PM				
6 PM				

Month: _____

	Friday	Saturday	Sunday	Note
07 AM				
08 AM				
09 AM				
10 AM				
11 AM				
12 PM				
1 PM				
2 PM				
3 PM				
4 PM				
5 PM				
6 PM				

Month: _____

	Monday	Tuesday	Wednesday	Thursday
07 AM				
08 AM				
09 AM				
10 AM				
11 AM				
12 PM				
1 PM				
2 PM				
3 PM				
4 PM				
5 PM				
6 PM				

Month: _____

	Friday	Saturday	Sunday	Note
07 AM				
08 AM				
09 AM				
10 AM				
11 AM				
12 PM				
1 PM				
2 PM				
3 PM				
4 PM				
5 PM				
6 PM				

Month: _____

	Monday	Tuesday	Wednesday	Thursday
07 AM				
08 AM				
09 AM				
10 AM				
11 AM				
12 PM				
1 PM				
2 PM				
3 PM				
4 PM				
5 PM				
6 PM				

Month: _____

	Friday	Saturday	Sunday	Note
07 AM				
08 AM				
09 AM				
10 AM				
11 AM				
12 PM				
1 PM				
2 PM				
3 PM				
4 PM				
5 PM				
6 PM				

Month: _____

	Monday	Tuesday	Wednesday	Thursday
07 AM				
08 AM				
09 AM				
10 AM				
11 AM				
12 PM				
1 PM				
2 PM				
3 PM				
4 PM				
5 PM				
6 PM				

Month: _____

	Friday	Saturday	Sunday	Note
07 AM				
08 AM				
09 AM				
10 AM				
11 AM				
12 PM				
1 PM				
2 PM				
3 PM				
4 PM				
5 PM				
6 PM				

Month: _____

	Monday	Tuesday	Wednesday	Thursday
07 AM				
08 AM				
09 AM				
10 AM				
11 AM				
12 PM				
1 PM				
2 PM				
3 PM				
4 PM				
5 PM				
6 PM				

Month: _____

	Friday	Saturday	Sunday	Note
07 AM				
08 AM				
09 AM				
10 AM				
11 AM				
12 PM				
1 PM				
2 PM				
3 PM				
4 PM				
5 PM				
6 PM				

Month: _____

	Monday	Tuesday	Wednesday	Thursday
07 AM				
08 AM				
09 AM				
10 AM				
11 AM				
12 PM				
1 PM				
2 PM				
3 PM				
4 PM				
5 PM				
6 PM				

Month: _____

	Friday	Saturday	Sunday	Note
07 AM				
08 AM				
09 AM				
10 AM				
11 AM				
12 PM				
1 PM				
2 PM				
3 PM				
4 PM				
5 PM				
6 PM				

Month: _____

	Monday	Tuesday	Wednesday	Thursday
07 AM				
08 AM				
09 AM				
10 AM				
11 AM				
12 PM				
1 PM				
2 PM				
3 PM				
4 PM				
5 PM				
6 PM				

Month: _____

	Friday	Saturday	Sunday	Note
07 AM				
08 AM				
09 AM				
10 AM				
11 AM				
12 PM				
1 PM				
2 PM				
3 PM				
4 PM				
5 PM				
6 PM				

Month: _____

	Monday	Tuesday	Wednesday	Thursday
07 AM				
08 AM				
09 AM				
10 AM				
11 AM				
12 PM				
1 PM				
2 PM				
3 PM				
4 PM				
5 PM				
6 PM				

Month: _____

	Friday	Saturday	Sunday	Note
07 AM				
08 AM				
09 AM				
10 AM				
11 AM				
12 PM				
1 PM				
2 PM				
3 PM				
4 PM				
5 PM				
6 PM				

Month: _____

	Monday	Tuesday	Wednesday	Thursday
07 AM				
08 AM				
09 AM				
10 AM				
11 AM				
12 PM				
1 PM				
2 PM				
3 PM				
4 PM				
5 PM				
6 PM				

Month: _____

	Friday	Saturday	Sunday	Note
07 AM				
08 AM				
09 AM				
10 AM				
11 AM				
12 PM				
1 PM				
2 PM				
3 PM				
4 PM				
5 PM				
6 PM				

Month: _____

	Monday	Tuesday	Wednesday	Thursday
07 AM				
08 AM				
09 AM				
10 AM				
11 AM				
12 PM				
1 PM				
2 PM				
3 PM				
4 PM				
5 PM				
6 PM				

Month: _____

	Friday	Saturday	Sunday	Note
07 AM				
08 AM				
09 AM				
10 AM				
11 AM				
12 PM				
1 PM				
2 PM				
3 PM				
4 PM				
5 PM				
6 PM				

Month: _____

	Monday	Tuesday	Wednesday	Thursday
07 AM				
08 AM				
09 AM				
10 AM				
11 AM				
12 PM				
1 PM				
2 PM				
3 PM				
4 PM				
5 PM				
6 PM				

Month: _____

	Friday	Saturday	Sunday	Note
07 AM				
08 AM				
09 AM				
10 AM				
11 AM				
12 PM				
1 PM				
2 PM				
3 PM				
4 PM				
5 PM				
6 PM				

Month: _____

	Monday	Tuesday	Wednesday	Thursday
07 AM				
08 AM				
09 AM				
10 AM				
11 AM				
12 PM				
1 PM				
2 PM				
3 PM				
4 PM				
5 PM				
6 PM				

Month: _____

	Friday	Saturday	Sunday	Note
07 AM				
08 AM				
09 AM				
10 AM				
11 AM				
12 PM				
1 PM				
2 PM				
3 PM				
4 PM				
5 PM				
6 PM				

Month: _____

	Monday	Tuesday	Wednesday	Thursday
07 AM				
08 AM				
09 AM				
10 AM				
11 AM				
12 PM				
1 PM				
2 PM				
3 PM				
4 PM				
5 PM				
6 PM				

Month: _____

	Friday	Saturday	Sunday	Note
07 AM				
08 AM				
09 AM				
10 AM				
11 AM				
12 PM				
1 PM				
2 PM				
3 PM				
4 PM				
5 PM				
6 PM				

Month: _____

	Monday	Tuesday	Wednesday	Thursday
07 AM				
08 AM				
09 AM				
10 AM				
11 AM				
12 PM				
1 PM				
2 PM				
3 PM				
4 PM				
5 PM				
6 PM				

Month: _____

	Friday	Saturday	Sunday	Note
07 AM				
08 AM				
09 AM				
10 AM				
11 AM				
12 PM				
1 PM				
2 PM				
3 PM				
4 PM				
5 PM				
6 PM				

Month: _____

	Monday	Tuesday	Wednesday	Thursday
07 AM				
08 AM				
09 AM				
10 AM				
11 AM				
12 PM				
1 PM				
2 PM				
3 PM				
4 PM				
5 PM				
6 PM				

Month: _____

	Friday	Saturday	Sunday	Note
07 AM				
08 AM				
09 AM				
10 AM				
11 AM				
12 PM				
1 PM				
2 PM				
3 PM				
4 PM				
5 PM				
6 PM				

Month: _____

	Monday	Tuesday	Wednesday	Thursday
07 AM				
08 AM				
09 AM				
10 AM				
11 AM				
12 PM				
1 PM				
2 PM				
3 PM				
4 PM				
5 PM				
6 PM				

Month: _____

	Friday	Saturday	Sunday	Note
07 AM				
08 AM				
09 AM				
10 AM				
11 AM				
12 PM				
1 PM				
2 PM				
3 PM				
4 PM				
5 PM				
6 PM				

Month: _____

	Monday	Tuesday	Wednesday	Thursday
07 AM				
08 AM				
09 AM				
10 AM				
11 AM				
12 PM				
1 PM				
2 PM				
3 PM				
4 PM				
5 PM				
6 PM				

Month: _____

	Friday	Saturday	Sunday	Note
07 AM				
08 AM				
09 AM				
10 AM				
11 AM				
12 PM				
1 PM				
2 PM				
3 PM				
4 PM				
5 PM				
6 PM				

Month: _____

	Monday	Tuesday	Wednesday	Thursday
07 AM				
08 AM				
09 AM				
10 AM				
11 AM				
12 PM				
1 PM				
2 PM				
3 PM				
4 PM				
5 PM				
6 PM				

Month: _____

	Friday	Saturday	Sunday	Note
07 AM				
08 AM				
09 AM				
10 AM				
11 AM				
12 PM				
1 PM				
2 PM				
3 PM				
4 PM				
5 PM				
6 PM				

Month: _____

	Monday	Tuesday	Wednesday	Thursday
07 AM				
08 AM				
09 AM				
10 AM				
11 AM				
12 PM				
1 PM				
2 PM				
3 PM				
4 PM				
5 PM				
6 PM				

Month: _____

	Friday	Saturday	Sunday	Note
07 AM				
08 AM				
09 AM				
10 AM				
11 AM				
12 PM				
1 PM				
2 PM				
3 PM				
4 PM				
5 PM				
6 PM				

Month: _____

	Monday	Tuesday	Wednesday	Thursday
07 AM				
08 AM				
09 AM				
10 AM				
11 AM				
12 PM				
1 PM				
2 PM				
3 PM				
4 PM				
5 PM				
6 PM				

Month: _____

	Friday	Saturday	Sunday	Note
07 AM				
08 AM				
09 AM				
10 AM				
11 AM				
12 PM				
1 PM				
2 PM				
3 PM				
4 PM				
5 PM				
6 PM				

Month: _____

	Monday	Tuesday	Wednesday	Thursday
07 AM				
08 AM				
09 AM				
10 AM				
11 AM				
12 PM				
1 PM				
2 PM				
3 PM				
4 PM				
5 PM				
6 PM				

Month: _____

	Friday	Saturday	Sunday	Note
07 AM				
08 AM				
09 AM				
10 AM				
11 AM				
12 PM				
1 PM				
2 PM				
3 PM				
4 PM				
5 PM				
6 PM				

Month: _____

	Monday	Tuesday	Wednesday	Thursday
07 AM				
08 AM				
09 AM				
10 AM				
11 AM				
12 PM				
1 PM				
2 PM				
3 PM				
4 PM				
5 PM				
6 PM				

Month: _____

	Friday	Saturday	Sunday	Note
07 AM				
08 AM				
09 AM				
10 AM				
11 AM				
12 PM				
1 PM				
2 PM				
3 PM				
4 PM				
5 PM				
6 PM				

Month: _____

	Monday	Tuesday	Wednesday	Thursday
07 AM				
08 AM				
09 AM				
10 AM				
11 AM				
12 PM				
1 PM				
2 PM				
3 PM				
4 PM				
5 PM				
6 PM				

Month: _____

	Friday	Saturday	Sunday	Note
07 AM				
08 AM				
09 AM				
10 AM				
11 AM				
12 PM				
1 PM				
2 PM				
3 PM				
4 PM				
5 PM				
6 PM				

Month: _____

	Monday	Tuesday	Wednesday	Thursday
07 AM				
08 AM				
09 AM				
10 AM				
11 AM				
12 PM				
1 PM				
2 PM				
3 PM				
4 PM				
5 PM				
6 PM				

Month: _____

	Friday	Saturday	Sunday	Note
07 AM				
08 AM				
09 AM				
10 AM				
11 AM				
12 PM				
1 PM				
2 PM				
3 PM				
4 PM				
5 PM				
6 PM				

Month: _____

	Monday	Tuesday	Wednesday	Thursday
07 AM				
08 AM				
09 AM				
10 AM				
11 AM				
12 PM				
1 PM				
2 PM				
3 PM				
4 PM				
5 PM				
6 PM				

Month: _____

	Friday	Saturday	Sunday	Note
07 AM				
08 AM				
09 AM				
10 AM				
11 AM				
12 PM				
1 PM				
2 PM				
3 PM				
4 PM				
5 PM				
6 PM				

Month: _____

	Monday	Tuesday	Wednesday	Thursday
07 AM				
08 AM				
09 AM				
10 AM				
11 AM				
12 PM				
1 PM				
2 PM				
3 PM				
4 PM				
5 PM				
6 PM				

Month: _____

	Friday	Saturday	Sunday	Note
07 AM				
08 AM				
09 AM				
10 AM				
11 AM				
12 PM				
1 PM				
2 PM				
3 PM				
4 PM				
5 PM				
6 PM				

Month: _____

	Monday	Tuesday	Wednesday	Thursday
07 AM				
08 AM				
09 AM				
10 AM				
11 AM				
12 PM				
1 PM				
2 PM				
3 PM				
4 PM				
5 PM				
6 PM				

Month: _____

	Friday	Saturday	Sunday	Note
07 AM				
08 AM				
09 AM				
10 AM				
11 AM				
12 PM				
1 PM				
2 PM				
3 PM				
4 PM				
5 PM				
6 PM				

Month: _____

	Monday	Tuesday	Wednesday	Thursday
07 AM				
08 AM				
09 AM				
10 AM				
11 AM				
12 PM				
1 PM				
2 PM				
3 PM				
4 PM				
5 PM				
6 PM				

Month: _____

	Friday	Saturday	Sunday	Note
07 AM				
08 AM				
09 AM				
10 AM				
11 AM				
12 PM				
1 PM				
2 PM				
3 PM				
4 PM				
5 PM				
6 PM				

Month: _____

	Monday	Tuesday	Wednesday	Thursday
07 AM				
08 AM				
09 AM				
10 AM				
11 AM				
12 PM				
1 PM				
2 PM				
3 PM				
4 PM				
5 PM				
6 PM				

Month: _____

	Friday	Saturday	Sunday	Note
07 AM				
08 AM				
09 AM				
10 AM				
11 AM				
12 PM				
1 PM				
2 PM				
3 PM				
4 PM				
5 PM				
6 PM				

Month: _____

	Monday	Tuesday	Wednesday	Thursday
07 AM				
08 AM				
09 AM				
10 AM				
11 AM				
12 PM				
1 PM				
2 PM				
3 PM				
4 PM				
5 PM				
6 PM				

Month: _____

	Friday	Saturday	Sunday	Note
07 AM				
08 AM				
09 AM				
10 AM				
11 AM				
12 PM				
1 PM				
2 PM				
3 PM				
4 PM				
5 PM				
6 PM				

Month: _____

	Monday	Tuesday	Wednesday	Thursday
07 AM				
08 AM				
09 AM				
10 AM				
11 AM				
12 PM				
1 PM				
2 PM				
3 PM				
4 PM				
5 PM				
6 PM				

Month: _____

	Friday	Saturday	Sunday	Note
07 AM				
08 AM				
09 AM				
10 AM				
11 AM				
12 PM				
1 PM				
2 PM				
3 PM				
4 PM				
5 PM				
6 PM				

Month: _____

	Monday	Tuesday	Wednesday	Thursday
07 AM				
08 AM				
09 AM				
10 AM				
11 AM				
12 PM				
1 PM				
2 PM				
3 PM				
4 PM				
5 PM				
6 PM				

Month: _____

	Friday	Saturday	Sunday	Note
07 AM				
08 AM				
09 AM				
10 AM				
11 AM				
12 PM				
1 PM				
2 PM				
3 PM				
4 PM				
5 PM				
6 PM				

Month: _____

	Monday	Tuesday	Wednesday	Thursday
07 AM				
08 AM				
09 AM				
10 AM				
11 AM				
12 PM				
1 PM				
2 PM				
3 PM				
4 PM				
5 PM				
6 PM				

Month: _____

	Friday	Saturday	Sunday	Note
07 AM				
08 AM				
09 AM				
10 AM				
11 AM				
12 PM				
1 PM				
2 PM				
3 PM				
4 PM				
5 PM				
6 PM				

Month: _____

	Monday	Tuesday	Wednesday	Thursday
07 AM				
08 AM				
09 AM				
10 AM				
11 AM				
12 PM				
1 PM				
2 PM				
3 PM				
4 PM				
5 PM				
6 PM				

Month: _____

	Friday	Saturday	Sunday	Note
07 AM				
08 AM				
09 AM				
10 AM				
11 AM				
12 PM				
1 PM				
2 PM				
3 PM				
4 PM				
5 PM				
6 PM				

Month: _____

	Monday	Tuesday	Wednesday	Thursday
07 AM				
08 AM				
09 AM				
10 AM				
11 AM				
12 PM				
1 PM				
2 PM				
3 PM				
4 PM				
5 PM				
6 PM				

Month: _____

	Friday	Saturday	Sunday	Note
07 AM				
08 AM				
09 AM				
10 AM				
11 AM				
12 PM				
1 PM				
2 PM				
3 PM				
4 PM				
5 PM				
6 PM				

Month: _____

	Monday	Tuesday	Wednesday	Thursday
07 AM				
08 AM				
09 AM				
10 AM				
11 AM				
12 PM				
1 PM				
2 PM				
3 PM				
4 PM				
5 PM				
6 PM				

Month: _____

	Friday	Saturday	Sunday	Note
07 AM				
08 AM				
09 AM				
10 AM				
11 AM				
12 PM				
1 PM				
2 PM				
3 PM				
4 PM				
5 PM				
6 PM				

Month: _____

	Monday	Tuesday	Wednesday	Thursday
07 AM				
08 AM				
09 AM				
10 AM				
11 AM				
12 PM				
1 PM				
2 PM				
3 PM				
4 PM				
5 PM				
6 PM				

Month: _____

	Friday	Saturday	Sunday	Note
07 AM				
08 AM				
09 AM				
10 AM				
11 AM				
12 PM				
1 PM				
2 PM				
3 PM				
4 PM				
5 PM				
6 PM				

Month: _____

	Monday	Tuesday	Wednesday	Thursday
07 AM				
08 AM				
09 AM				
10 AM				
11 AM				
12 PM				
1 PM				
2 PM				
3 PM				
4 PM				
5 PM				
6 PM				

Month: _____

	Friday	Saturday	Sunday	Note
07 AM				
08 AM				
09 AM				
10 AM				
11 AM				
12 PM				
1 PM				
2 PM				
3 PM				
4 PM				
5 PM				
6 PM				

Month: _____

	Monday	Tuesday	Wednesday	Thursday
07 AM				
08 AM				
09 AM				
10 AM				
11 AM				
12 PM				
1 PM				
2 PM				
3 PM				
4 PM				
5 PM				
6 PM				

Month: _____

	Friday	Saturday	Sunday	Note
07 AM				
08 AM				
09 AM				
10 AM				
11 AM				
12 PM				
1 PM				
2 PM				
3 PM				
4 PM				
5 PM				
6 PM				

Month: _____

	Monday	Tuesday	Wednesday	Thursday
07 AM				
08 AM				
09 AM				
10 AM				
11 AM				
12 PM				
1 PM				
2 PM				
3 PM				
4 PM				
5 PM				
6 PM				

Month: _____

	Friday	Saturday	Sunday	Note
07 AM				
08 AM				
09 AM				
10 AM				
11 AM				
12 PM				
1 PM				
2 PM				
3 PM				
4 PM				
5 PM				
6 PM				

Month: _____

	Monday	Tuesday	Wednesday	Thursday
07 AM				
08 AM				
09 AM				
10 AM				
11 AM				
12 PM				
1 PM				
2 PM				
3 PM				
4 PM				
5 PM				
6 PM				

Month: _____

	Friday	Saturday	Sunday	Note
07 AM				
08 AM				
09 AM				
10 AM				
11 AM				
12 PM				
1 PM				
2 PM				
3 PM				
4 PM				
5 PM				
6 PM				

Month: _____

	Monday	Tuesday	Wednesday	Thursday
07 AM				
08 AM				
09 AM				
10 AM				
11 AM				
12 PM				
1 PM				
2 PM				
3 PM				
4 PM				
5 PM				
6 PM				

Month: _____

	Friday	Saturday	Sunday	Note
07 AM				
08 AM				
09 AM				
10 AM				
11 AM				
12 PM				
1 PM				
2 PM				
3 PM				
4 PM				
5 PM				
6 PM				

Month: _____

	Monday	Tuesday	Wednesday	Thursday
07 AM				
08 AM				
09 AM				
10 AM				
11 AM				
12 PM				
1 PM				
2 PM				
3 PM				
4 PM				
5 PM				
6 PM				

Month: _____

	Friday	Saturday	Sunday	Note
07 AM				
08 AM				
09 AM				
10 AM				
11 AM				
12 PM				
1 PM				
2 PM				
3 PM				
4 PM				
5 PM				
6 PM				

Month: _____

	Monday	Tuesday	Wednesday	Thursday
07 AM				
08 AM				
09 AM				
10 AM				
11 AM				
12 PM				
1 PM				
2 PM				
3 PM				
4 PM				
5 PM				
6 PM				

Month: _____

	Friday	Saturday	Sunday	Note
07 AM				
08 AM				
09 AM				
10 AM				
11 AM				
12 PM				
1 PM				
2 PM				
3 PM				
4 PM				
5 PM				
6 PM				

Month: _____

	Monday	Tuesday	Wednesday	Thursday
07 AM				
08 AM				
09 AM				
10 AM				
11 AM				
12 PM				
1 PM				
2 PM				
3 PM				
4 PM				
5 PM				
6 PM				

Month: _____

	Friday	Saturday	Sunday	Note
07 AM				
08 AM				
09 AM				
10 AM				
11 AM				
12 PM				
1 PM				
2 PM				
3 PM				
4 PM				
5 PM				
6 PM				

Month: _____

	Monday	Tuesday	Wednesday	Thursday
07 AM				
08 AM				
09 AM				
10 AM				
11 AM				
12 PM				
1 PM				
2 PM				
3 PM				
4 PM				
5 PM				
6 PM				

Month: _____

	Friday	Saturday	Sunday	Note
07 AM				
08 AM				
09 AM				
10 AM				
11 AM				
12 PM				
1 PM				
2 PM				
3 PM				
4 PM				
5 PM				
6 PM				

Month: _____

	Monday	Tuesday	Wednesday	Thursday
07 AM				
08 AM				
09 AM				
10 AM				
11 AM				
12 PM				
1 PM				
2 PM				
3 PM				
4 PM				
5 PM				
6 PM				

Month: _____

	Friday	Saturday	Sunday	Note
07 AM				
08 AM				
09 AM				
10 AM				
11 AM				
12 PM				
1 PM				
2 PM				
3 PM				
4 PM				
5 PM				
6 PM				

Month: _____

	Monday	Tuesday	Wednesday	Thursday
07 AM				
08 AM				
09 AM				
10 AM				
11 AM				
12 PM				
1 PM				
2 PM				
3 PM				
4 PM				
5 PM				
6 PM				

Month: _____

	Friday	Saturday	Sunday	Note
07 AM				
08 AM				
09 AM				
10 AM				
11 AM				
12 PM				
1 PM				
2 PM				
3 PM				
4 PM				
5 PM				
6 PM				

Month: _____

	Monday	Tuesday	Wednesday	Thursday
07 AM				
08 AM				
09 AM				
10 AM				
11 AM				
12 PM				
1 PM				
2 PM				
3 PM				
4 PM				
5 PM				
6 PM				

Month: _____

	Friday	Saturday	Sunday	Note
07 AM				
08 AM				
09 AM				
10 AM				
11 AM				
12 PM				
1 PM				
2 PM				
3 PM				
4 PM				
5 PM				
6 PM				

Month: _____

	Monday	Tuesday	Wednesday	Thursday
07 AM				
08 AM				
09 AM				
10 AM				
11 AM				
12 PM				
1 PM				
2 PM				
3 PM				
4 PM				
5 PM				
6 PM				

Month: _____

	Friday	Saturday	Sunday	Note
07 AM				
08 AM				
09 AM				
10 AM				
11 AM				
12 PM				
1 PM				
2 PM				
3 PM				
4 PM				
5 PM				
6 PM				

Printed in Great Britain
by Amazon